Cover: "Witch Hill" or "The Salem Martyr"
Thomas Slatterwhite Noble, 1869
Oil on canvas.

Witchcraft At Andover

by
Sarah Loring Bailey

taken from *Historical sketches of Andover,
comprising the present towns of
North Andover and Andover.*

SicPress 2012
Methuen, Mass.

"Witchcraft at Andover" is an excerpt from *Historical sketches of Andover, comprising the present towns of North Andover and Andover* by Sarah Loring Bailey, published in Boston in 1880.

The principal authorities consulted for this account, are The Essex County Court Papers, Mass. Archives, Woodward's Copies of Court Papers, Drake's Annals, Upham's Salem Witchcraft, Calef's and Mather's Accounts, Historical Collections, Assistants' Records, Suffolk County Court Papers.

series edited by J. Godsey
for copies sales@SicPress.com
Methuen, MA 2012

WITCHCRAFT AT ANDOVER

The fiftieth anniversary of Andover's settlement (1692) was destined to be a year of peculiar trial and distress. At the opening of the year, it seemed that the town might reasonably hope to enjoy a season of prosperity. There were no near alarms of hostile Indians; the church controversies, which had been a source of trouble, were settled; there was nothing, apparently, to hinder the growth or disturb the peace of the community. But a cloud was gathering which was to bring darkness and desolation, a convulsion heaving that threatened to break up the very foundations of society. Few persons, who have not made the subject a special study, have an adequate conception of the magnitude of this calamity of the witchcraft delusion. It is often said that too much stress has been laid upon it; the number who suffered death was small, the pains of their execution were as a drop in the ocean compared with the sufferings of thousands slain for conscience in other countries and other communions. It is not, however, by numerical computations that the magnitude of the crisis can be estimated and the peril to the community and to the Puritan church appreciated. What made the peculiar danger of this panic was its creation of universal distrust. Every man doubted whether his neighbor, his minister, his friend, the wife of his bosom, the children of his household, were not of those given over to Satan, sold to the service of the enemy of souls. And in his very doubt, querying whether or no such terrible suspicion could have foundation in truth, the suspecter finds himself suspected, arrested, hurried to jail, brought to trial, sentenced to death; his protestations unheeded, his denials pronounced obstinacy, his prayers blasphemy and imprecation. The insecurity of all institutions, domestic and social, in such a state of things is apparent. If the examinations and trials had been conducted by any ordinary processes and according to any rules of evidence, there might have been a hope of arriving at truth. But the character of the witnesses, the nature of their testimony, the methods of their examination, — all tended to increase rather than allay the excitement. The examiners proceeded on the assumption that the accused were guilty; they invited evidence against them, in their zeal almost put words into the mouths of reluctant confessors and faltering witnesses, and they placed implicit faith in every statement corroborative of their preconceived opinions. Not that these men, some of the best and most conscientious of their time, delighted in the punishments inflicted or did not grieve for the necessity laid upon them. What made the situation most hope- less was that the magistrates were, as they believed, "verily doing God service," engaging for the sake of Christ's kingdom in a contest with the Prince of Evil, — a contest in which at every cost they must persist and conquer; though to do so they should be forced to sacrifice all which they held dearest. At least, such seems to the writer of this history the character and motives of the men who prosecuted the trials and advocated severity. But, whatever our estimate of the actors in the tragedy, the acts themselves are of thrilling interest, bringing to view in most prominent parts the men and women and even the children of our town.

A belief in witchcraft was everywhere prevalent at the period of the colonial settlements. That Satan often worked through human agency to perform wonders was almost an essential article of the theological dogmas of the time, and this doctrine was surrounded and overlaid with many vulgar traditions and superstitions. Now and then, in the course of controversies and litigations, especially among the illiterate classes of society, accusations would be brought against persons, of malicious connivings with the devil, to injure their opponents by Satanic arts. Such a charge was brought in 1658 against one John Godfrey of Andover. The principal sufferer from his wiles was the wife of Job Tyler of Boxford, who attended the church and was one of the taxpayers of Andover. The charge was brought in connection with a lawsuit of Haverhill men against Godfrey for non-payment of a debt, but seems not to have been satisfactorily established, and Godfrey subsequently brought suit for defamation. With John Godfrey's lawsuit, the craft of witches seems to have ceased, and even at this time not to have much disturbed the community; the minister, Rev. Francis Dane, giving decided opinion against its probability.

The beginning of "the witchcraft" proper was in the winter of 1691, in Salem village (Danvers). Some young girls were in the habit of meeting together for entertainment, — games, amusements, such as were permitted to young people. They tried sleight-of-hand, tricks of fortune-telling, looking into the palm of the hand and reading the future of the person's life by the interlacing lines there visible, as has been a custom of the credulous from that day to the present. The old historians call this "practising palmistry." Filling their minds with thoughts of this sort; they became fascinated and wonder-stricken, in talking about the supernatural. Ghosts, hobgoblins, devils, were the theme of their story-telling, and the subjects of their imaginings by night and by day. Some of them soon began to see strange sights, hear voices, dream dreams. They consulted an old Indian fortune-teller, gifted in wonder-working; some of them began to be seized with convulsions, and to experience physical contortions of various sorts; the others caught the infection. They vied with each other in strange exhibitions, their conduct having become a subject of general notice and curiosity and of scientific or theological study. Stimulated and excited, they were wrought up to every species of hysterical manifestation; they barked and mewed; they wriggled themselves off into corners under tables; they did all frenzied acts, which the human mind, left a prey to morbid and unbridled imaginations, can invent. Their bodies, too, showed strange and inexplicable marks of torture and violence. Purple spots, as of bruises or violence from human hands, marks of teeth, prickings of pins, were visible on them; they grew emaciated, and had the appearance of being the victims of a wasting disease. The physicians could not cure them, and, as was not uncommon, suggested that they were under the affliction of an evil spirit. The ministers then made their case a subject of special prayer. Eminent clergymen from Boston were summoned. Pre-eminent among them was the Rev. Cotton Mather, a zealous investigator and curious, "entertained," as he phrases it, in considering these morbid manifestations. The unanimous conclusion was, that the unhappy victims were afflicted of the devil. This view of their case was communicated to the girls, and did not tend to alleviate their sufferings. Whether these were real or feigned, due wholly to diseased fancies, or were, in the case of any, sheer hypocrisy and of malice contrived, opinions differ. The sufferers, either of their own accord or by suggestion, intimated that their sufferings were caused by some persons in the community through whose agency Satan worked to torture them. The persons whom they at first selected for accusation were two or three poor vagrant creatures, objects of common contempt or charity, — a terror to children, such forlorn souls as almost every village had when asylums and alms-houses were few. These half-crazed and outcast wretches were readily believed to be guilty of the sin charged upon them. They were tried with more or less satisfactory results. Others than they were soon accused; the wonder grew; whenever a person had any disease which baffled medical skill, these afflicted girls, who were supposed to have clairvoyant power, or "spectre-evidence," as to the cause of sickness, were consulted. They usually pronounced the cause of the sickness to be due to the affliction of some person, — "witchcraft."

It chanced, in the spring of 1692, that the wife of Joseph Ballard, of Andover, having long been ill, and having found no relief in medicine, her husband became anxious to try the spiritual method of ascertaining the cause of her ailment. Accordingly, he sent to Salem and brought two of the girls to Andover. One who came was Ann Putnam, of Salem. These girls were received with great solemnity, taken to the meeting-house, and, prayer having been made by the Rev. Mr. Barnard (Mr. Dane seems to have kept aloof from the proceedings, which was perhaps the reason of suspicion's falling on him and his family), they were adjured to tell the truth.

They named certain persons of Andover and other places as the tormentors of the sick woman. John Ballard, the constable, forthwith obtained a warrant for the arrest of the accused, and hurried them off to Salem jail. They, being plied with questions as to their accomplices and partners in guilt, named others, who also followed them to jail, till, in about three months, some forty or more were under arrest, and lying in irons, manacles, and fetters (all these instruments are mentioned in the records) in the crowded and miserable jail. The consternation and excitement of the community were beyond bounds. The belief gained ground that the devil had made a plot to destroy the Christian faith in the community and win over the people to himself. These men and women, fathers and mothers of Andover, — and their innocent children, — were thought to have sold themselves and their families to him. It was said he had made them sign their names in blood in his book, and bind themselves to do his bidding for a term of years: "Did wickedly, maliciously and feloniously covenant with the devil, did signe the Devils Book with Blood, did give himself soul and body to the Devil, by which wicked and diabolical covenant he is bound a Detestable Witch," is the form of indictment found against the prisoners, from children of eight years old to men and women gray-headed, parents and grandparents. Many confessed the charge to be true; said the devil had baptized them in the Shawshin River, or in Five-mile Pond, on whose borders they held midnight meetings, stealing out of their houses and riding through the air on sticks, going as far as Salem village, the gathering-ground of witches. These stories, creations of a diseased imagination, were implicitly believed by the friends and relatives of the accused, at least by many. Instead of directing their efforts to calm the frenzied mind and restore to right reason their unhappy friends, near and dear kindred joined their voices to those of the magistrates and ministers, begging the accused to make full confession.

One of the saddest features of the delusion was that it held for nothing the former high character of the accused. At first, it is true, only the friendless and the strange, eccentric persons in the community or the high-tempered, or those who for any bold stand had incurred spite or made enemies, were selected. But, an epidemic of audacity seemed at length to seize the afflicted. One of the "higher powers" accused, and the magic circle broken, which birth, social position, and religious character had at first put their barriers around, a rivalry seems to have begun who should " bring out " (as was said) the most improbable and unsuspected of guilt. The sort of vulgar satisfaction, which rejoices in the degradation, and humiliation of those above its own level, now reveled in reducing the pride of the lofty. Into the most honored households, the tongue of accusation thrust itself, and fastened its venomous touch upon the purest and gentlest there. The ladies who had walked hitherto as examples in the community, the admired, but the envied of many, were brought low. Mistress Mary Osgood, and the wife of the deacon of the church, Mrs. Eunice Frye, a woman of all Christian virtues, and the Rev. Mr. Dane's daughter, Mrs. Abigail Faulkner, and her innocent children, Dorothy and Abigail Faulkner, and another of Mr. Dane's daughters, Elizabeth Johnson, and her daughter, "Elizabeth Johnson Jr.," and Mr. Dane's daughter-in-law, Mrs. Deliverance [Hazeltine] Dane, were accused; and finally, Mr. Dane himself was hinted at, Mrs. Dudley Bradstreet named, and Mr. Dudley Bradstreet compelled to seek safety in flight. Such was the frenzy which seized the community and loosed its basest and most dangerous passions. The people clamored for trial and punishment of the accused, as they always clamor when superstition or suspicion of crime is rife, and each thinks to prove his own innocence by zeal for his fellows' conviction of guilt.

In the trials, eight citizens of Andover were condemned. Three of these were hanged: Martha Carrier, Samuel Wardwell, Mary Parker; one died in prison, Ann Foster; Abigail Faulkner was reprieved, and by the delay ultimately saved; Sarah Wardwell and Elizabeth Johnson and Mary Lacey were condemned at the very latest trial, January, 1692-3, and set free on the general jail delivery, when the frenzy was checked. The following is a list of those names of the accused, which have been found[1], and the various identifying notes in regard to them:

>Barker, Abigail, wife of Ebenezer Barker, not guilty.
>Barker, Mary, single woman, daughter of John Barker, not guilty.
>Barker, William, Snr., brother of John Barker, not guilty.
>Bridges, Mary, single woman, not guilty.
>Bridges, Mary, wife of John Bridges, not guilty.
>Bridges, Mary, Jr., aged twelve years, daughter of John Bridges.
>Bridges, Sarah, single woman, afterward wife of John Preston, not guilty.
>Carrier, Martha [Allen], wife of Thomas Carrier, hanged.
>Carrier, Andrew, son of Thomas Carrier.
>Carrier, Richard[2], son of Thomas Carrier.
>Carrier, Thomas, son of Thomas Carrier.
>Carrier, Sarah, age seven years, daughter of Thomas Carrier.
>Dane, Deliverance, wife of Nathaniel Dane.
>Draper, John.
>Farrington, Edward.
>Faulkner, Abigail, wife of Francis Faulkner, sentenced.
>Faulkner, Dorothy, ten years, daughter of Francis Faulkner.
>Faulkner, Abigail, eight years, daughter of Francis Faulkner.
>Foster, Ann, mother of Abraham Foster, condemned (died in prison).
>Frye, Eunice, wife of Dea. John Frye, not guilty.
>Fawkes, Sarah, single woman, afterward wife of Francis Johnson, not guilty.
>Johnson, Elizabeth [Dane], wife of Stephen Johnson, mother of Francis Johnson.
>Johnson, Elizabeth, Jr., sister of Francis Johnson, condemned.

---

[1] *Nehemiah Abbot was of Topsfield — sometimes named of Andover.*
[2] *A Richard Carrier, son of Andrew Carrier, is mentioned.*

Johnson, Abigail, eleven years, sister of Francis Johnson.
Johnson, Stephen, thirteen years, brother of Francis Johnson.
Johnson, Rebecca, widow, mother of John Johnson.
Lacey, Mary [Foster], wife of Lawrence Lacey, condemned.
Lacey, Mary, Jr., daughter of Lawrence Lacey.
Osgood, Mary, wife of Capt. John Osgood.
Parker, Mary, mother of Joseph Parker, hanged.
Parker, Sarah.
Post, Mary, of Boxford[1], daughter of Rebecca Johnson, condemned.
Sawdey, John, apparently an apprentice.
Tyler, Mary, wife of Hopestil Tyler, not guilty.
Tyler, Johanna, daughter of Hopestil Tyler.
Tyler, Hannah, single woman, not guilty.
Wardwell, Samuel, hanged.
Wardwell, Sarah, wife of Samuel Wardwell, condemned.
Wardwell, Mercy, daughter of Samuel Wardwell, not guilty.
Wilson, Sarah, wife of Joseph Wilson.
Wilson, Sarah, daughter of Joseph Wilson.

The above marked "not guilty" were those on whom verdict was pronounced at the court which sat January, 1692/3 (1693). The others were perhaps not all formally tried. "Examinations," so-called, in which many confessed, preceded the trials and the evidence of the witnesses. Besides the above names, some others were reckoned with Andover. Rebecca Eames of Boxford, was one. The reason of this was that the Andover deputy to the General Court received the restitution money ultimately allowed to their legal representatives for losses. In the examinations of the accused, which preceded the regular trial, most made confession and thus averted the extreme penalty. Martha Carrier was the only one of all, male or female, who did not at some time or other, make an admission or confession. From the first moment to the last, under all the persuasions and exhortations of friends, under denunciations and threats of the magistrates and examiners, she held firm, denying all charges, and neither overborne in mind nor shaken in nerve, met death with heroic courage.

[1] *Often mentioned as of Andover..*

The charge of witchcraft was not the first of Martha Carrier's troubles; indeed, the former may have been in a sense the cause of the later affliction. The Carrier family, who came to Andover from Billerica [they were living in the latter town about 1685], were not welcome residents. Thomas Carrier was of Welsh birth, say the earlier historians. He seems to have been blessed with a comfortable temperament, for not-withstanding the misfortunes which befell him as a husband and father in the course of these witchcraft trials: his wife hanged, his sons imprisoned and cruelly handled, his daughter of tender years accused and made to confess against her mother, — sorrows enough to have brought some men to a pre-mature grave, — he lived to the age of one hundred and nine years, his head not bald nor his hair gray, and of such bodily activity that he walked[1] six miles a few days before his death.

The wife, Martha Allen, was a resident of Andover before her marriage, the daughter of Andrew Allen, Snr. Her sister Mary was married to Roger Toothaker of Ipswich and Billerica, and her nephew, Allen Toothaker, was a resident of Andover. The family were obnoxious, and were warned out of the town, because they had the small-pox, as appears from the following extract from the town records:

> To Samuel Holt, Andrew Allen and John Allen, Neighbors and friends:
>
> We the subscribers of Andover have been informed that your sister Carrier and some of her children are smitten with that contagious disease the small-pox and some have been soe inconsiderate as to think that the care of them belongs to the salact men of Andover which does not, for they took care when first they came to towne to warne them out again and have attended the law therein : and shall only take care that they doe not spread the distemper with wicked carelessness which we are afraid they have already done : you had best take what care you can about them, nature and Religion requiring of it. We hope we have done faithfully in this information and are your friends and servants.
>
> Dated 14th Oct. 1690

---

[1] *Abbot's History of Andover, 1829*

Later the selectmen issue the following warrant to the constable to provide for their support and the safety of the town:—

> To Walter Wright Constable: Whereas it has pleased God to visit those of the widdowe Allen's family which she hath taken into her house with that contagious disease the small-pox, it being as we think part of our duty to prevent the spreading of sd distemper we therefore requier you in their Majesties' names to warn sd family not to goe near any house soe as to endanger them by sd infection nor to come to the public meeting till they may come with safety to others : but what they want let them acquaint you with: which provide for them out of their own estates.
> Dated the 4:9. 1690.

These intruders who made so much trouble would not be likely to suffer last or least when witchcraft was supposed to be abroad. Martha Carrier was, too, a woman of a disposition not unlikely to make enemies: plain and outspoken in speech, of remarkable strength of mind, a keen sense of justice, and a sharp tongue. She, doubtless (from all that appears), took largely upon herself the care of the household, and no small interest in the management of the out-of-door affairs, in which she sometimes came into collision with the neighboring farmers. If the stories of witnesses can be credited (they were, it is plain, in some instances, greatly exaggerated) she had more than once threatened vengeance upon persons who, as she thought, over-reached and cheated her husband in his bargains. Among her unguarded speeches was brought against her, that she had declared "she would stick as close as the bark of a tree" to Benjamin Abbot (who had a dispute with her and her husband about laying out land), and he "should repent his conduct afore seven years came to an end," and "she would hold his nose so close to the grindstone as ever it was held since his name was Benjamin Abbot." As this man soon after had a swelling on his foot, and "a paine in his side which bred a sore that discharged several gallons of corruption," he was convinced that Martha Carrier had bewitched him. She was also accused of witchcraft exercised upon some of the afflicted girls of Salem, and on complaint of Joseph Houlton and John Walcott, of Salem, a warrant was issued for her arrest May 28, 1692. She was the first arrested at Andover, so far as record is found. John Ballard, the constable, carried her off, and as soon as she was gone Benjamin Abbot " began to mend and grew better every day," as the witnesses in the trial averred, until he was quite well.

On the 31st of May the prisoner underwent an examination; being confronted with the persons who claimed to be suffering from her, five women and children of Salem and vicinity:

"Abigail Williams, who hurts you? Goody Carrier of Andover.

"Elizabeth Hubbard who hurts you? Goody Carrier.

"Susan Sheldon who hurts you? Goody Carrier; she bites me, pinches me, and tells me she would cut my throat, if I did not sign her book."

These are specimens of the questioning, and the sort of answers, which it elicited. The witnesses were seized with fits as soon as she looked at them, and "fell into the most in-tolerable outcries and agonies," as the chroniclers of the time relate. They said they saw a black man standing beside her. She denied that she knew anything of what they affirmed, and her manner was so defiant, as the magistrate thought, that it proved conclusively her guilt and impenitence. "I see the souls of thirteen persons whom she has murdered at Andover," cried one of the accusers. Goaded to desperation at this foul charge, the exasperated woman exclaimed, "You lie; I am wronged!" then turning to the magistrates she boldly made appeal and rebuke: "It is false; and it is a shame for you to mind what these say, that are out of their wits!" But the accusers persisted that they saw the black man, and that even then the prisoner was practising diabolical arts upon them, and their tortures seemed (and doubtless were) so great that, as the records say, "there was no enduring it." So she was " ordered away and to be bound hand and foot with all expedition, the afflicted in the meanwhile almost killed to the great trouble of all spectators, magistrates and others." Thus handcuffed and fettered she was put into jail, where also her sons and her little daughter were soon incarcerated, to await further trial. A summons for witnesses was issued July 30:

> Wm & Mary by ye Grace of God of England, Scotland, France &; Ireland King & Queen Defend of ye faith &c. ss. To ye Constable or Constables of Andover Greeting.
>
> Wee Comand you to Warn and give Notice unto Allen Toothaker, Ralph Farnum junr, John Farnum son of Ralph Farnum Snr, Benjamin Abbot and his wife, Andrew Foster, Phebe Chandler daughter of William Chandler, Samuel Holt Snr, Samuel Preston Jnr., that they and every one of them be and personally appear at ye Court of Oyer and Terminer to be held by adjournment on Tuesday next at Ten of ye Clock in ye Morning there to testifye ye truth to ye best of their knowledge on certain indictments to be exhibited against Martha Carrier of Andover; hereof fail not at your utmost perill and make return of your doings herein. Stephen Sewall, Clerk.
>
> Dated in Salem July 30th 1692.

Of the examination of Martha Carrier, Upham says:

> The examination of Martha Carrier must have been one of the most striking scenes of the whole drama. The village meeting-house presented a truly wild and exciting spectacle; the fearful and horrible superstition, which darkened the minds of the people, was displayed in their aspect and movement. Their belief that then and there, they were witnessing the great struggle between the kingdom of God and of the Evil One and that everything was at stake on the issue gave an awe-struck intensity to their expression. The blind unquestioning confidence of the magistrates, clergy, and all concerned in the prosecutions, in the evidence of the accused, the loud outcries of their pretended sufferings, their contortions, swoonings, and tremblings excited the usual consternation in the assembly. In addition to this, there was the more than ordinarily bold and defiant bearing of the prisoner, stung to desperation by the outrage upon her poor children; her firm and unshrinking courage, facing the tempest that was raised to overwhelm her, sternly rebuking the magistrates: "It is a shameful thing that you should mind these folks that are out of their wits," her whole demeanor proclaiming her conscious innocence, and proving that she chose chains, the dungeon, and the scaffold rather than to belie herself. Seldom has a scene in real life, or a picture wrought by the inspiration of genius and the hand of art in its individual character or its general grouping surpassed that presented on this occasion.

After two months imprisonment in the heat of midsummer, the unhappy woman was brought out on the first of August to face the neighbors and relations who were summoned to bear testimony. One and all they testified against her, — that she had afflicted them in their persons and estates, causing diseases to fall upon them and their cattle, and blight upon their crops. But, notwithstanding all the accumulation of evidence, she was undaunted and firm in maintaining her innocence. Others might confess to save themselves, or, because by so much evidence and argument they were driven to the belief that in some mysterious way they were actually, though unconsciously working with the devil, and drawn into his toils; but Martha Carrier's strong, clear mind no sophistry could bewilder, and her intrepid courage no threats terrify. The Rev. Cotton Mather was shocked at her impiety and her obduracy. An "arrant hag" he calls her, and says that as a reward of her adherence to Satan she had received the promise that she should be "queen of hell." He also says that even her own sons testified against her; but it appears from a letter written by one of their fellow prisoners that this confession was extorted from them by violence, which reminds us of the tortures of the Spanish Inquisition : "The sons of Martha Carrier would not confess anything till they had tied them neck and heel till the blood was ready to come out of their noses."

The little girl, Sarah Carrier, was brought into court August 11, 1692. There is something peculiarly touching in the scene, — this simple child, before the assembled magistrates and dignitaries, arraigned on a charge which she could not in the least comprehend, and confessing to the vagaries and overwrought fancies excited in her childish mind by fear, or prompted by the suggestions of her interrogators:

    "How long hast thou been a witch?"
    "Ever since I was six years old."
    "How old are you now?"
    "Near eight years old; brother Richard says I shall be eight years old in November."

"Who made you a witch?"
"My mother. She made me set my hand to a book."
"How did you set your hand to it?"
"I touched it with my fingers and the book was red and the paper of it was white."
"You said you saw a cat once. What did the cat say to you?"
"It said it would tear me in pieces, if I did not set my hand to the book"
"How did you know that the cat was your mother?"
"The cat told me that she was my mother."

With such absurd notions was the mind of the child filled by the grave and reverend magistrates and ministers, of whom it now seems impossible to conceive that they could have seriously put these questions about cats' talking, and a woman's assuming the form of a cat to delude her own child. Yet these were men who, in the ordinary affairs of life, were sensible and sagacious. If the facts teach anything, it certainly is a lesson of human fallibility.

Several women of Andover who confessed, accused Martha Carrier as the cause of their being led into witchcraft. Three of these were, Ann Foster, her daughter Mary Lacey, and her granddaughter, Mary Lacey, Jr. Ann Foster said she rode on a stick with Martha Carrier to Salem village, that the stick broke and she saved herself by clinging around Martha Carrier's neck. She said they met three hundred witches at Salem village, among them the Rev. Mr. Burroughs, and another minister with gray hair (Mr. Dane, of Andover, was supposed to be hinted at). This story was confirmed by the daughter and the granddaughter. Besides these ridiculous charges, there were others, which had more foundation in truth. All the events of Martha Carrier's past life were gone over, and her rash speeches and revengeful words brought up, with some facts, which looked greatly against her. Long ago, as one witness testified, she, angry with him, "gave forth several threatening words as she often used to doe," and, "soon after, the deponent found one of his large lusty sowes dead near Carrier's house, and one of his cowes which used to give a good Mess of milk would give little or none." Said the witness, John Roger:

> "I did in my conscience believe then in ye day of it and have so done ever since and doe yet believe that Martha Carrier was ye occasion of those ill accidents by means of Witchcraft; she being a very malicious woman."

Her nephew, Allen Toothaker, testified that "he had lost a three year old heifer, next a yearlin and then a cow and he knew not of any naturall causes of ye death of the above sd creatures, but have always feared it hath been ye effect of my aunt Carrier's her malice."

Samuel Preston had also lost a cow, after Martha Carrier had a difference with him. In all these cases the witnesses deposed that she had threatened these losses.

Phebe Chandler, eleven years old, testified:

> "About a fortnight before the prisoner was sent for to Salem, ye upon ye Sabbath day when ye psalm was singing sd Martha Carrier took me by ye shoulder &; shaked me in ye meeting-house & asked me where I lived but I made her no answer, not doubting but that she knew me, having lived some time the next door to my father's house[1] on our side of the way."

She also said further, in relation to the prisoner's poisoning her:

> "That day that sd Martha Carrier was accused my mother sent me to carry some beer to ye folks ye were att work in ye lott & when I came within Carriers ye fence, there was a noise in ye bushes which I thought was Martha Carriers voice (which I knew well) but I saw nobody & ye voice asked me what I did there &; whither I was going which greatly frighted me."

She goes on to say that she heard a voice again telling her that she would be poisoned in two or three clays. And so it was,

---

[1] *In the south part of the town, on the road from Ipswich to Billerica, lived William Chandler, Snr.*

her right hand swelled, and she had "a great weight on her breast and pain in her leges." When she got better, and went to meeting, Richard Carrier looked upon her "and the pains returned and she was struck deaf and heard none of ye prayers."

"During the trial one of the afflicted," says Cotton Mather, "had her hands unaccountably tied together with a wheel-band, so fast that without cutting it could not be loosened." This was said to be done by the spectre or evil spirit working with and through Martha Carrier.

The prisoner was hanged August 19, 1692, along with four men, among them the Rev. George Burroughs. They were carried in a cart through the streets of Salem, crowds thronging to see the sight. Even from the scaffold, Martha Carrier's voice was heard asseverating her innocence[1]. Her dead body was rudely treated, thrust into the ground in the same hole or grave with the bodies of Mr. Burroughs and John Willard. Calef describes the burial:

> When he (Mr. Burroughs) was cut down, he was dragged by a halter to a hole or grave between the rocks about two feet deep; his shirt and breeches being pulled off and an old pair of trousers of one executed put on his lower parts; he was so put in together with Willard and Carrier that one of his hands and his chin and a foot of one of them was left uncovered.

Nothing more is found recorded of Martha Carrier, till, in the year 1711, her name occurs on a list of sufferers, whose legal representatives received money for losses sustained by the imprisonment and death of their relations. Seven pounds six shillings was allowed to the representatives of Martha Carrier. Some persons received fifty pounds. This has been commented on as an unjust and partial discrimination; but it appears to have been simply according to the claim presented for money expended or loss incurred. Some families, whose friends

---

[1] *"All of them said they were innocent, Carrier and all." — Account of the Execution in the Diary of Judge Sewall. Mass. Hist. Soc. Coll., Fifth Series, vol. V. 14*

were long in prison and during the winter, were at great expense to provide them with comforts, and some had property seized as forfeited to the government, on the ground that it was the estate of a condemned criminal; some, also, were at expense in caring for the bodies of their friends and rescuing them from an ignominious burial.

To compensate friends for the greatest wrong done, the moral one, or to make reparation for the outrages inflicted on the innocent and defenceless prisoners, or the cruelty to their families of giving their bodies to the hangman, was not contemplated in the Acts of the General Court for "Reversal of Attainders and Restitution for Losses." For such wrongs and losses, the deepest and most real, done to individuals, governments offer no redress.

In regard to the other woman of Andover who was hanged, no particulars are found recorded. Several facts go to prove that she was the widow of Joseph Parker, who had been of a somewhat "distempered mind," and incapable of the care of her estate. The following petition tells her story in brief:

> Whereas our honored mother was Imprisoned and upon her Tryal was condemned for supposed witchcraft upon such evidence as is now generally thought to be insufficient and suffered the Pains of Death at Salem in the year 1692 we being well satisfied not only of her innocency of that crime that she was condemned for, but of her piety humbly desire that the attainders may be taken off, that so her name that has suffered may be restored.

The sons of Mary Parker also show in their petition that after their mother's execution an officer sent by the sheriff came to Andover to seize her estate. The sons told him that she left no estate. Whereupon he seized their cattle, corn, and hay, and threatened that their estate should be sold, unless they could make a contrary agreement with the sheriff. They were therefore obliged to make a journey to Salem and expend much money to save their property from sale. They claimed eight pounds restitution.

In the trial of Mary Parker, she was accused by Mercy Wardwell and by William Barker (who both confessed to be witches), of joining with them to afflict one Timothy Swan of Andover. Several persons were also in the presence of the Court restored by the touch of her hand. On such evidence she was sentenced.

Samuel Wardwell was hanged September 22, 1692. He at his first examination had confessed, but in a short time re-canted his confession. He did this in the spirit of martyrdom, saying that he had once "belyed himself," but that he begged forgiveness for it, and though he knew that to persist in his recantation would cost him his life he would hold to the truth. Two indictments were found against him. The first of these was as follows:

> .... That Samuel Wardwell of Andover in the County of Essex, carpenter on or about the fifteenth day of August in the yeare aforesaid and divers other days and times as well before as after, certain detestable arts called witchcraft and sorceries, wickedly malitiously and feloniously hath used practised and exercised at and in the Towne of Boxford in the County of Essex in and upon and against one Martha Sprague of Boxford in the County of Essex aforesaid single woman; by which said wicked Arts the said Martha Sprague of Boxford in the County of Essex aforesaid, the day and yeare aforesaide and divers other days and times both before and after was and is tortured, afflicted. Consumed, Pined, wasted and Tormented and also for sundry other acts of witchcraft by the said Samuel Wardwell comited and done before and since that time against the peace of our Sovereign Lord and Lady the King and Queen their Crowne and dignity. And the form in the Statute in that case made and Provided.

In the second indictment it was presented that about "Twenty yeares agoe in the Town of Andover, he the said Samuel Wardwell with the evil speritt, the Devil a covenant did make, wherein he promised to honor, worship and believe the devil contrary to the statute of King James the First in that behalfe made and Provided, etc."

The witnesses against him were Martha Sprague[1] and several girls, also three prominent men of Andover, Joseph Ballard, Ephraim Foster, Thomas Chandler.

The last was a man sixty-five years old, of much experience in affairs, civil and military. His testimony shows how cautious the more practical and sensible men were in regard to their utterances about the witchcraft:

> The testimony of Thomas Chandler aged about sixty-five, who saith that I have often heard Samuel Wardwell of Andover tell young persons their fortune and he was much adicted to that and mayd sport of it, and further saith not.

Here again in the accused we see one of those odd geniuses, or wonder-loving characters, of whom every community has some always, who deal in the marvellous, tell great stories, dupe the credulous to the amusement of the crowd, and who, in an age of superstition, were apt to claim a knowledge of future events, and who, perhaps, believed in a measure in their own supernatural gifts.

Ephraim Foster seemed to put some faith in his townsman's prophecies. He testified that Wardwell had made some predictions in regard to the birth of his (Foster's) children, that there would be five girls in the household before a son should be born. This had proved true. The witness had also often seen Wardwell "tell fortins," and he observed that in doing so the fortune-teller always " looked first into the hand of the person, and then cast his eyes down on the ground." This was proof of his being in league with Satan, though the connection is not obvious.

Wardwell himself confessed that he was guilty of covenanting with the devil. He said it was on this wise: Some years ago he

---

[1] *"Alias Tyler."*

had "fallen into a discontented state of mind because he was in love with a maid named Barker who slighted his love." While thus melancholy, one day, being behind Mr. Bradstreet's house, he saw "some cats together." One of these cats, as he related, "assuming the form of the black man," spoke to him, promising that " he should live comfortably and be a captain"[1] if he would sign the book. He was induced to make the signature, and was baptized in the Shawshin River, where "he was dipt all over, and renounced his former baptism."

In his recantation of this confession, the prisoner gave as his reason for ever making such a statement, that the examiners had insisted that he was a servant of the devil, and had urged him to name the time when he made the covenant; and being thus driven to specify the time, he had persuaded himself there must have been such a time, and he had gone back to this period of dejection as the only one in which he was likely to have done the deed. It would seem as though he and the others who confessed were unsettled in their own right reason and judgment by the many voices against them, the over-whelming evidence, and the importunities of the examiners that they would confess, and searching back over their past lives for some consciously or unconsciously-made covenant, found it in circumstances of mental depression or bodily suffering, the remembrance of which became clouded with phantoms conjured up by the fears of the hour. Nor would it be strange that a person, especially, who had so often exercised the pretended gift of fortune-telling, should half suspect himself of being under the power of supernatural beings. Even in the materialism of the nineteenth century, the mystery is not all solved, of those at least almost preternatural powers which some persons seem to have in certain abnormal conditions. It cannot, therefore, be much wondered at that the simple-minded fortune-teller of the seventeenth century, in old Andover, when his minister and all the

---

[1] *Captains then were the chief men, — as Captain Bradstreet, owner of the house near the scene of temptation.*

most devout magistrates told him he was a witch, should, temporarily at least, believe that he was.

But it shows that he had, in spite of all his odd ways, more strength of character and real principle than might at first be supposed, that he did not long remain thus obscured as to his estimate of himself. At the last, although he knew that his only hope of safety was in adhering to his confession, he wholly denied its truth. His mind, once cleared, became strong, and steady, and his statements true and consistent.

On the gallows he protested his innocence. While he spoke, the wind blew a puff of smoke from the executioner's pipe into his face. The accusers exclaimed: "The devil doth hinder his words!"

Seven other persons were hanged at the same time with Wardwell. The Rev. Mr. Noyes, pointing to the bodies, addressed the crowd with a moral: "What a sad thing it is to see eight firebrands of hell hanging there!"

The account presented by the sons of Samuel Wardwell shows that there was taken by the government to pay the expenses of his trial and execution the following:

Five cowes	£10 0 0
One heifer and a yearling	2 5 0
Nine hogs	7 0 0
Eight loads of hay	4 0 0
A set of carpenter's tools	1 10 0
Six acres of corn upon the ground	9 0 0
	£36 15s

Another who was condemned was Ann Foster. She, however, was not hanged, having died in the prison before the law could take its course. She was an aged woman, a widow, without friends of influence to give aid in her distress. She was evidently weak in mind and body, and was ready at the trial to confess almost anything, and believe everything which was suggested against herself. Indeed, some of these women had been so long used to contemplate their natural and acquired depravity, in its most aggravated forms, that some of the sensitive and self-accusing were ready, even in their ordinary religious meditations, to regard themselves as guilty of almost all sin, believing literally that "he that offendeth in one point is guilty of all." The piety of Ann Foster is especially spoken of by her sons, and there can be little doubt that she was led to charge herself with the sin of witchcraft in all sincerity and contrition. A broken-down old woman in her decrepitude and weakness, torn from her quiet home, brought on a long journey to a prison and a court-room, accused of blaspheming her God and forsaking her Saviour, — what wonder if she sank and died under such a weight of miseries. She was four times examined, — July 15th, 16th, 18th, 21st. It is pitiful to think of this poor, tottering, feeble creature, dragged again and again before her accusers, and finally dismissed to the sheriff to be "taken care of" as guilty.

She overdid in confession, or she would, like the others, have doubtless been saved. But the law must have victims, and here was one who proved herself to be deeply guilty. She confessed that she bewitched a hog of John Lovejoy's, caused the death of one of Andrew Allen's children, made another child sick, and "hurt" Timothy Swan. She said her manner of hurting was to make images of the persons with rags ("poppets" they are called in the records), and stick pins in these, or "tye knots in the rags," or burn them in the fire. The persons whom these images were supposed to represent would suffer whenever she pinched or burned, or pricked the "poppet."

The deluded woman also described extraordinary apparitions which she had seen, — birds, with great eyes, which first were white and became black when they flew away, by which she knew they were devils, also black men who were devils. She had been at the witch-meetings and seen the Rev. George Burroughs and another minister with gray hair. Again and again, she repeated and owned this confession. But on one point she was obstinate. She would accuse herself to any extent, but she would not accuse her daughter. For this her examiners lost patience with her. "You have been already three times examined," they exclaim, "and yet you do not confess" — that is, she did not confess to making her daughter a witch; even though the daughter admitted that she was one and charged it upon her mother's influence and agency:

> "Your daughter was with you and Goody Carrier when you did ride upon the stick?"
> "I did not know it."
> "How long have you known your daughter to be engaged."
> "I cannot tell nor have I any knowledge of it at all."
> "Do you not acknowledge that you did so?"
> "No and I know no more of my daughter's being a witch than what day I shall die upon."
> "You cannot expect peace of conscience without a free confession."
> "If I knew anything more, I would speak of it to the utmost."

But in spite of this denial the daughter alleged that it was true that they were both witches, and she cried out: "O mother, we have left Christ and the devil hath got hold of us!" he distressed mother moving her lips in prayer was asked what she was doing, and replied that she was "praying to the Lord." "What Lord? said the examiners sternly, "What God do witches pray to?" Thus taunted and overborne, the harassed woman in confusion and distraction exclaimed: "I cannot tell; the Lord help me!"

The granddaughter confirmed her mother's statements that they were both witches, made so by the prisoner. The story of Ann Foster is graphically told in a petition presented by her son. It was written by some abler pen than his, for he only made his mark:

> To The Honorable Committee now Sitting at Salem:
> Whereas my mother Ann Foster of Andover suffered imprisonment twenty-one weeks and upon her Tryall was condemned for supposed witchcraft upon such evidence as now is Generally thought Insuf-

ficient and died in prison, I being well persuaded of my mother's innocence of the crime for which she was condemned I humbly desire that the attainder may be taken off. The charges and expenses for my mother during her imprisonment is as follows:

> The money which I was forced to pay the keeper before I could have the dead body of my mother to bury her was £2 10s
> Money and provisions
> Expended while She was in prison   £4
> Total expenses   £10

This sum of money the petitioner received, and also for his sister Mary Lacey £8 10s, on petition and by order of her husband Lawrence Lacey.[1]

Mrs. Abigail Faulkner was sentenced to death, but, by the intercession of friends, delay was obtained, and finally she was set free, when orders were given for a general release. Her trial is one of the most noteworthy. She was the daughter of the minister who for forty-five years had lived in Andover, and she was the first who had been condemned in the town of those in high social standing. Her conduct in the courts was worthy of her position, free alike from credulous weakness on the one hand and from scornful defiance on the other. Either from her own good sense, or upheld by the wise counsels of her father (who never yielded to the delusion), she showed the greatest discretion, paying due deference to the court, yet never losing her firmness and dignity. That she was not to be intimidated by superstitious terrors, the examiners knew, it is evident, for they forbore to argue with her about "peace and judgment to come," but they urged her to confess, "for ye credit of her Towne! " This seems almost to have a spice of malice and meanness in it, at all events to be very shrewd to bring about the desired end, for to hint even that the fair name of the town was to suffer from the family of the minister was not to help him who had recently been involved in difficulties with his parishioners.

---

[1] Mass. Archives, "Witchcraft Petitions."

However, the daughter had her father's spirit, and even this innuendo, if it were one, did not move her. She merely made reply in the dignity of simple truth, that "God would not require her to confess that she was not guilty of." Still later, when witnesses were numerous and evidence overwhelming, she made admissions, guardedly, and as if with the design of conceding, all that could be conceded with a view to appeasing the clamor for her confession. She admitted it was possible that the devil might be working through her, but if so she was not conscious of it and did not consent to it. She explained some of the charges against her by saying, that when so many of her relations had been accused she had been " raised in her spirit " [that is, excited and indignant], and al- most frantic, and she "had pinched her hands together" in her distress. The examiners had charged that by this "pinching of her hands" the afflicted were tortured. She admitted that possibly it was so, but yet it was not she who hurt them, but the devil working through her without her knowledge or consent. It was noted against her that she was unmoved by the sufferings of the afflicted; though she said she was sorry for them " she did not shed a tear." Some seven or eight charged upon her their tortures. Added to the distress of so many accusers was the greatest of all, that of having her two little girls (eight and ten years old) confess themselves witches and charge their mother with being their teacher. Also, Martha Tyler, Johanna Tyler, Sarah Wilson, and Joseph Tyler, confessing themselves witches, "did all acknowledge that they were led into that dreadful sin of witchcraft by the means of the aforesd Abigail Faulkner."

She was kept in prison thirteen weeks, and when set free, by the general "jail delivery," was legally liable to penalty. In the year 1700, she presented a memorial to the General Court praying for the defacing of the record against her, by which she was under the attainder of a convicted criminal:

"I am as yet suffered to live, but only as a malefactor convicted upon record of ye most heinous crimes that mankind can be sup- posed to be guilty of, which besides its utter ruining and defaming my Reputation will certainly expose myself to Imminent Danger by new accusations which will thereby be the more readily believed will remain a perpetual brand of infamy upon my family. I do humbly pray that the High and Honourable Court will please to take my case into serious consideration and order the Defacing of ye record against me, so that I may be freed from ye evil consequences thereof."

Not until after eleven years, and much petitioning, was the attainder taken off. The record remains to this day one of the most conspicuous on the pages of the "Book of Witchcraft," in the State Archives. Its clear and distinct writing, among many nearly illegible papers, make it one of the noticeable records; so that even the casual turner of the leaves cannot fail to read it:

The Jury find Abigail Faulkner
wife of Francis Faulkner of Andover
GUILTY OF Ye FELONY OF WITCHCRAFT
Comited on ye body of Martha Sprague
also on ye body of Sarah Phelps
SENTENCE OF DEATH PASSED ON ABIGAIL FAULKNER.
Copia vera.

The niece of Abigail Faulkner, granddaughter of Mr. Dane and daughter of Stephen and Elizabeth Dane Johnson, Elizabeth Johnson Jnr., Was also condemned and reprieved, and thereby saved (Mr. Dane and his friends using every effort to stop the tide of superstition, and finally succeeding), A petition of the brother of Elizabeth Johnson attests the fact of her condemnation:

To THE HONOURABLE COMMITTEE SITTING AT SALEM Sept 3, 1710.

Whereas my sister Elizabeth Johnson, Jr. of Andover was imprisoned six months for ye supposed witchcraft and upon her Tryall was condemned by such evidence as is now generally thought to be Insufficient in the year 1692 She the said Elizabeth Johnson humbly prays that the attainder may be taken off.

My experiences for maintaining my sister with provisions during her imprisonment was £3. 0. 0. which I pray may be allowed

by FRANCIS JOHNSON — in behalf of my sister.

Again, in 1712, the petitioner makes request, her name having by some mistake been omitted from the list of those named in the Reversal of Attainder, October 17, 1711:

> WHEREAS THE HONBLE GENERAL COURT hath lately made an act for taking off the attainder of those that were condemned for witchcraft in the year 1692, I thought meet to inform your Honors that I was condemned by the Court at Salem in January in the year 1692 as will appear by the Records of the Tryals at said Court, but my name is not inserted in said act. Being very desirous of the favour of that act am bold humbly to pray your Honors to represent my case to the General Court at their next Session that my name may be inserted in that act; if it may be and that the Honourable Council would please to allow me some-thing in consideration of my charges by reason of my long imprisonment which will be thankfully acknowledged as a great favor by your Honors most humble servant
>
> ELIZABETH JOHNSON, Jnr. [1]
>
> Andover Feb 19 1711-12.

Elizabeth Johnson's confession ought to have saved her from condemnation, if, as some persons argued, confession implied penitence, and penitence was salvation from the penalty of the law. She owned to everything charged. It would seem that the few verdicts of guilty rendered at the trials of January 1692-3, when the reaction of feeling had set in, were merely formal. The confession of Elizabeth Johnson was that Goodwife Carrier persuaded her, and she had been baptized in Goodwife Carrier's well by the devil. He "dipt her head over in water." She had been at witch-meeting, and seen bread and wine at the devil's sacrament. She had afflicted many persons by poppets. She had some poppets made of rags, and some of "birch Rhine" [bark.?]. She afflicted Ann Putnam "with a speare of iron." She showed red spots on her body, where she said her "familiar," the evil spirit, sucked her.

Mary Lacey, daughter of Ann Foster, was condemned. She said the devil had carried her in his arms to Newbury falls, and

---

[1] *Elizabeth Johnson, Jr., and Mary Lacey, Jr., were, it would seem, young persons under parental authority.*

there he had baptized some of the "higher powers." She also said (to use the words of the deposition) "if she doe but take a ragg, clout or any such thing and roll it up together and imagine it to represent such and such a person, then whatsoever she doth to that Rag or clout so rouled up the person represented thereby will be in lyke manner afflicted."

The trials and confessions are so similar that repetition is needless.

Sarah Wardwell, wife of Samuel Wardwell, was found guilty at the Court of Trials, January 2, 1693. The record[1] of the verdict is as follows:

> A jury being called, Nathan Howard foreman and accordingly sworne, the jury went out to agree on their verdict, who returning did then and there in open court deliver their verdict that the said Sarah Wardwell was Guilty of covenanting with the Devill for which she stood Indicted in the first Indictment as also Guilty of the ffelony by witchcraft, for which she stood indicted in the second Indictment.

The sons of Samuel and Sarah Wardwell petitioned for restitution, and especially to have their mother's name inserted in the list of those whose attainder was taken off by the Act of Reversal:

> Whereas my mother Sarah Wardel was condemned by the Court at Salem some time in January in the year 1692 (Jan. 1695) as I suppose will appear by the Records of the Tryalls at that Court, but her name is not inserted in the late Act of the Generall Court for the taking of the attainder off those that were condemned in that year, my mother being since deceased I thought it my duty to endeavor that her name may have the Benefit of the Act:
>
> I mentioned only what was seized of my father's estate by the sheriffe, but gave no account of other charges which did arise from the imprisonment of my Father and Mother; they having provided for their own subsistence, while they were in Prison, and I suppose there was something considerable payd to the keeper of the Prison, though I am not able now to give a particular account how much it was. If your Honors

---

[1] *Suffolk County Records — "Assistant's Records."*

please to allow me something upon that account it will be thankfully acknowledged by your honors most humble servant

SAMUEL WARDEL.

Feb 19 1711-12

What was the condition of the young children of Samuel and Sarah Wardwell, their father hanged and their mother in prison, we learn from a record of the selectmen of Andover, part of which also is recorded in the "Essex County Court Papers":

> Wee ye subscribers selectmen of Andover ye above sd year, having informed ye Quarter Sessions at Ipswich ye 27th of ye aboves September that there was severall children of Sam Wardwels ye was in a suffering condition begging their advice direction & order therein which they were pleased to Consider of & order as followes ye ye Selectmen for ye time being should place out, or if need require binde out s" children in good & honest families, referring to a law in that case provided. Persuant to this order of ye Court wee have placed them as follows; viz Samuel Wardwell we placed with John Ballard his uncle for one year, William we placed with Corpl Saml Frie till he come to be of ye age of one and twenty years; sd Frie to learne him ye trade of a weaver. Eliakim we placed to Daniel Poor till he was twenty-one years of age &; Elizabeth we placed with John Stevens till eighteen years of age, all ye above sd were to find them with suites of apparel att ye end of sd term of tyme.
>
> SAML FRIE
> JOHN ASLEBE   SELECTMEN
> JOHN ABBOT

Of the prisoners tried and acquitted, one of those highest in standing was Elizabeth Dane, wife of Stephen Johnson. She suffered five months' imprisonment. Her daughter Elizabeth, as has been said, was condemned, and her daughter Abigail, and her son Stephen, were accused and imprisoned five weeks. Her son Francis Johnson, received restitution-money in her behalf.

The boy Stephen Johnson was thirteen years of age. He did (in the words of the indictment) "wickedly, maliciously &; feloniously with the devil a covenant make, wherebye he gave himselfe soule and body to the Devil and signed the Devils Booke with his blood and by the devil was baptized and renounced his Christian baptism, by which wicked &; Diabolical covenant with the Devil made the said Stephen Johnson is bound a detestable witch," etc

Mary Marston, wife of John Marston, made a full confession, that one evening, when she was alone in the house, the black man came in and offered her a paper book to sign, which she did sign with a pen dipped in ink, "and therewith made a Strooke."

She accused William Barker of joining with her to afflict.

William Barker, examined August 29th, confessed that, being a poor man, and having a large family, and unable to pay his debts, he signed the devil's book, Satan agreeing to pay all his debts, and give him a comfortable life. He said that the world hitherto had " gone hard with him."

Mercy Wardwell, Richard Carrier, and others, also confessed. The most remarkable confession was that of Mrs. Mary Osgood, the wife of Mr. John Osgood. She was a woman of exemplary character, and had always been respected and beloved in the community. Yet, though of unblemished life and incapable of falsehood, as every one believed, she now confessed that for eleven years she had been devoted to the service of Satan; she had prayed to the devil instead of to God; she had been baptized by the devil in Five-mile Pond; she had taken many midnight journeys through the air, in company with Deacon Frye's wife, and Ebenezer Barker's wife, and Goody Tyler; she had expected to have great satisfaction in the devil's service, but he had never given it to her, and she was miserable. Her husband testified that he believed in the truth of her statements. The principal evidence, besides her own confession, against Mrs. Osgood, was that of Goody Tyler. But what that was worth, and how it was extorted, may be learned from a second confession, or recantation, made by this woman to the Rev. Increase Mather. This minister, less credulous than his son, and also probably enlisted in the cause of, and laboring with, the Rev. Francis Dane and others, to bring about a reaction of feeling and save the prisoners, the kinsfolk and parishioners of Mr, Dane, visited the Andover women in the prison, and obtained counter-confessions. The reasons for the first confessions he states, as given him by the women themselves:

> Goodwife Tyler did say that when she was first apprehended she had no fears upon her and did think that nothing could have made her confess against herself. But, since she hath found to her great grief that she had wronged the truth and falsely accused herself.

The account goes on to say that, on the way from Andover to Salem, her brother Bridges rode with her, and told her that it must be that she was a witch, because the afflicted were raised out of their fits at her touch. She constantly denied and begged him not to urge her to confess. After she got to Salem, she was carried into a room where her "brother on one side and Mr. John Emerson on the other side " did tell her she was certainly a witch, and Mr. Emerson said he could see the devil before her eyes, and with his hands "tried to beat him away from her eyes!' And they "so urged her to confess that she wished herself in any dungeon rather than be so treated. Well, I see you will not confess. Well I will now leave you and then you are undone body and soul forever."

They told her that in confessing "she could not lie," to which she answered, "Good brother, do not say so, for I shall lie, if I confess, and then who shall answer unto God for my lie." They said she would surely be hanged if she did not confess; that God would not suffer so many good men to be in error, and that she surely was a witch. She told Mr. Mather "that they continued so long and so violently to urge and press her to confess, that she thought verily her life would have gone from her," and at last she said, "almost everything that they propounded to her."

She told Mr. Mather, also, that "she wronged her conscience in so doing," was "guilty of a great sin in belying of herself and desired to mourn for it so long as she lived." This she said, and "a great deal more of the like nature" (as the clergyman relates), "and all with such affliction, sorrow, relenting, grief and mourning that it exceeds any pen to describe and express the same."

Mrs. Osgood likewise explained to Mr. Mather the way in which she was led to confess. She said that the examiners asked her at what time she became a witch. She told them she did not know. They said she did know and she must tell, and thus beset she considered, that " about twelve years before when she had her last child she had a fit of sickness and was melancholy and so thought that time might be as proper a time to mention as any and accordingly did prefix the said time."

She explained her saying that the devil appeared to her, by relating that the examiners told her the devil did appear, and pressed her to say in what shape, and remembering that just before her arrest she saw a cat, she "at length did say it was in the shape of a cat. Not as though she in any whit suspected the said cat to be the devil in the day of it, but because some creature she must mention, and this came into her mind at the time."

It will be noticed, in considering these examinations and confessions, that it was not the least conscientious, the least scrupulous in morals, who uttered the seeming falsehoods and perjuries. It was the religiously brought up, the shrinking women and children, accustomed to rely implicitly on the judgment and advice of their superiors in worldly wisdom, or in theological learning. Martha Carrier, having no importunate advisers begging her not to ruin herself and them, and being used to depend on her own judgment, stood firm, the sole one of forty or more who did not make an admission of complicity or agency in the devil's works, and who did not indeed even admit (what the wisest believed) that there was Satanic agency in the matter,

Abigail Faulkner, who made only partial admissions, acted no doubt under the instructions of her father, who saw that only concession of some points would save her, and could advise it conscientiously, since neither he nor any one else could know for a certainty that the devil was not concerned in these extraordinary manifestations.

Some of the accused were examined by Mr. Dudley Bradstreet, Justice of the Peace, at Andover, August 10, 1692. He seems to deprecate the necessity laid upon him, and to disclaim any judgment in the matter. He evidently, though humane and not so credulous as many in regard to the wild stories current, had not the determination and strength that characterize the minister, Mr. Dane. His letter to the magistrates and examiners, relating what action he took, is as follows[1]:

> GENTLEMEN: I thought it meet to give you this broken account hoping it may be of some service. I am wholly unacquainted with affairs of this nature neither have the benefit of books for forms &c; but "being unadvisedly entered upon service I am wholly unfit" for beg that my ignorance and failings may be as much covered as conveniently may be which will ever be acknowledged by your poor and unworthy servant.
>
> I know not whether to make any returns. Bonds I have taken. The Custos rotulorum I know not, ...
>
> To THE HONORED BARTHOLOMEW GEDNEY, JOHN HATHORNE, ESQ., or any of their Majesties Justices of the Peace in Salem these humbly present.

The condition of the women and children of Andover, delicately reared as some of them had been, and used to the comforts of as luxurious homes as could be found in new in- land plantations, now thrust with all sorts of prisoners into the common jail at Salem, was pitiable indeed. Many of them were six months in prison, and some even eight months[2]. Their sufferings were great in the heat of summer, and with the approach of winter it seemed probable that they would be extreme. To pro-

---

[1] *Mass, Hist. Soc. Coll., Third Series, vol. i*

[2] *Rebekah Johnson, who was the sexton of the North Church (the only woman appointed by the town to take care of the Meeting-house), was in jail eight months.*

cure, if possible, some alleviation of their misery, their friends petitioned[1] for their release from jail, under bonds, before winter should set in:

> To THE HONOURED COURT NOW SITTING IN BOSTON this 12th of October 1692. Right Honoured Gentlemen and Fathers, We, your humble petitioners, whose names are underwritten, petition your honors as followeth : We would not trouble you with a tedious Diversion, but briefly spread open our distressed condition and beg your honour's favor and pity in affording what relief may be thought convenient. As for the matter of our Troubles it is the distressed condition of our wives and Relations in prison at Salem who are a company of poor distressed creatures as full of inward grief and trouble as they are able to bear up in life withall. And besides the agrivation of outward troubles and hardships they undergo and want of food; and the coldness of the winter season that is coming may soon despatch such out of the way that have not been used to such hardships.
>
> And besides this, the exceeding great charges and expences that we are at upon many accounts which will be Tedious to give a particular account of, which will fall heavy upon us, especially in a time of so great charge and expence upon a general account in the country, which is expected of us to bear a part as well as others, which if all put together our families and estates will be brought to Ruin, if it cannot in time be prevented. Having spread open our condition, we humbly make our address to your Honors, to Grant that our Wives and Relations (being such that have been approved as penitent Confessors), might be returned home to us upon what bond your honors may see good. We do not petition to take them out of the hand of Justice, but to remove them as Prisoners under bonds in their own families where they may be more tenderly cared for and be ready to appear to answer further when the Honored Court shall call for them. We humbly crave your Honors favor and pitty for us and ours. Having set down our Troubled State before you, we hereby pray your honors:
>
>> JOHN OSGOOD in behalf of his wife.
>>
>> JOHN FRY in behalf of his wife.
>>
>> JOHN MARSTON in behalf of his wife Mary Marston.
>>
>> CHRISTOPHER OSGOOD in behalf of his daughter Mary Marston.
>>
>> JOSEPH WILSON in behalf of his wife & children.

[1] *Mass. Archives, vol. cxxxv., page 59.*

JOHN BRIDGES in behalf of his wife & children.
HOPE TYLER in behalf of his wife & daughter.
EBENEZER BARKER for his wife.
NATHANIEL DANE for his wife.

This petition was accompanied by another of about the same date, October 18th, from the ministers and other inhabitants of Andover. The name of Dudley Bradstreet is not among the signatures to it; the reason being that he was now under suspicion or accusation, had fled the town, and was living secreted in hope the storm would blow over. The allusion in the petition to "more of our neighbors of good reputation," doubtless points to Colonel Dudley Bradstreet, and the petitions were intended to operate in his favor by turning the tide of public feeling, so that he might venture to appear.[1] The following is the full text of the petition:

> We being deeply sensible of the heavy judgment that the Righteous God hath brought upon this place thought it our duty (after our earnest prayers to the God of Heaven to give us help from our trouble) to lay before this Honourable Assembly our present distressed state and to crave a redress of our grievances. It is well known that many persons of this town have been accused of witchcraft, by some distempered persons in these parts[2] and upon complaint made have been apprehended and committed to prison. Now, though we would not appear as advocates for any who shall be found guilty of so horrid a crime, but we heartily desire that this place and the whole land may be purged from that great wickedness, yet if any of our friends and neighbors have been misrepresented, as is possible some of them have been, we would crave leave (if it might be without offence) to speake something in their behalf, having no other design therein than that the truth may appear. We can truly give this Testimony of the most of them belonging to this town that have been accused that they never gave the least occasion as we hear of to their nearest relations or most intimate acquaintances to suspect them

---

[1] *Mass. Archives, vol. cxxxv., page 61.*
[2] *This, it will be noted, is strong language and high ground to take, to charge the persons as being distempered, when in the popular and the theological judgment the afflicted were gifted with supernatural powers of seeing the cause of diseases and those who caused their own affliction.*

of witchcraft. Several of the women that are accused were members of the church in full communion, and had obtained a good report for their blameless conversation and their walking as becometh women professing godliness; but whereas it may be alledged that the most of our people that have been apprehended for witchcraft have upon examination confessed it. To which we answer that we have nothing to plead for those that freely and upon conviction own themselves guilty; but we apprehend the case of some of them to be otherwise; for from the information we have had and the discourse some of us have had with the Prisoners, we have reason to think that the extream urgency that was used with some of them by their friends and others who privately examined them, and the fear they were then under hath been an inducement to them to own such things as we cannot since find they are conscious of. And the truth of what we now declare we judge will in time more plainly appear. And some of them have exprest to their neighbors that it hath been their great trouble that they have wronged themselves and the truth in their confessions.

We are also very sensible of the distressed condition of several poor families on whom this great trouble is fallen. Some of our neighbors are likely to be impoverished or ruined by the great charge they are at to maintain such of their families as are in Prison, and by the fees that are demanded of them, whose case we pray may be considered.

Our troubles which have hitherto been great we foresee are likely to continue and increase; if other methods be not taken than as yet have been; for there are more of our neighbors of good reputation and integrity who are still accused and we know not who can think himself safe, if the accusation of children and others who are under Diabolicall influence shall be received against persons of good fame.[1]

The petition[2] is signed with twenty-six names: Francis Dane, Snr.; Thomas Barnard; John Osgood; Thomas Johnson, and others. A letter,[3] written about the same time by Mr. Brattle of Boston, giving a "Full and Candid Account of the Delusion called Witchcraft," shows that this was the date of Mr. Bradstreet's seclusion and also rehearses in full the story of "poor Andover" It is perhaps the fullest contemporary account

---

[1] *The charge of being under the influence of Satan, it will be noted, is here brought against the accusers, and it had the designed effect in reversing the popular sentiment.*

[2] *Essex County Court Records.*

[3] *Mass. Hist. Soc. Collections*

of the delusion in this town. It is not improbable that Mr. Dane's influence had something to do with its writing:

Oct. 8, 1692.

.... This consulting of these afflicted children about their sick was the unhappy beginning of the unhappy troubles at poor Andover. Horse and man were sent to Salem village from the said Andover for some of the said afflicted and more than one or two of them were carried down to see Ballard's wife and to tell who it was that did afflict her. I understood that the said B. took advice before he took this method but what pity was it that he should meet with and hearken to such bad counsellors. Poor Andover does now rue the day that ever the afflicted went among them; they lament their .folly and are an object of great pity and commiseration. Capt. B. and Mr. St. [Stevens (?)] are complained of by the afflicted, have left the town and do abscond. Deacon Fry's wife, Capt. Osgood's wife and some others remarkably pious and good people in repute are apprehended and imprisoned and that which is more admirable the forementioned women are be- come a kind of confessors, being first brought thereto by the urgings and arguings of their good husbands, who having taken up that corrupt and highly pernicious opinion that whosoever were accused by the afflicted were guilty did break charity with their dear wives upon their being accused and urge them to confess their guilt, which so far prevailed with them as to make them say they were afraid of their being in the snare of the devil and which through the rude and barbarous methods (you may possibly think that my terms are too severe, but should I tell you what a kind of. blade was employed in bringing these women to their confessions; what methods from damnation were taken; what violence used; how unseasonably they were kept up; what buzzings and chuckings of the head were used and the like, I am sure that you would call them as I do rude and barbarous methods) that were afterward used at Salem, issued in somewhat plainer degrees of confession and were attended with imprisonment : The good deacon and Captain are now sensible of the error they were in; do grieve and mourn bitterly that they should break their charity with their wives and urge them to confess themselves witches. They now see and acknowledge their rashness and uncharitableness and are very lit objects for the pity and prayers of every good Christian. Now I am writing concerning Andover I cannot omit the opportunity to send you this information, that whereas there is a report spread abroad the country how that they were much addicted to sorcery in the said town and that there were forty men in it that could raise the devil as well as any astrologer and the like; after the best search that I can make into it, it proves a mere slander and a very unrighteous imputation.

The Rev. Elders[1] of the said place were much surprised upon their hearing of the said report and faithfully made inquiry about it, but the whole of naughtiness that they could discover and find out was only this that two or three girls had foolishly made use of the sieve and scissors as children have done in other towns. This method of the girls I do not justify in any measure; but yet I think it very hard and unreasonable that a town should lie under the blemish and scandal of sorceries and conjuration merely for the inconsiderate practices of two or three girls in the said town. But although the chief judge and some of the other judges be very zealous in these proceedings yet this you may take for a truth that there are several about the Bay, men for understanding, judgment and piety inferior to few if any in New England that do utterly condemn the said proceedings and do deliver their judgment in the case to be this that these methods will utterly ruin and undo poor New England. I shall nominate some of these to you.

Among the magistrates whom he names as disapproving the action of the Court of Oyer and Terminer in the trials was the "Hon. Simon Bradstreet our Late Governor."

The petition made of the Andover people seems not to have had the desired effect to secure the removal of the prisoners to their homes.

On the sixth of December, another petition was made by several inhabitants of Andover saying that their "wives have been exposed to great sufferings which daily increase by reason of the winter coming on and they are in extream danger of perishing, and the petitioners beg that their friends may be permitted to come home on such terms as your honors may judge meet." They offer to give bonds for the appearance of the prisoners whenever called for. This appeal and the sufferings of the prisoners could hardly fail to move compassion. Toward the last of December, the work of removing the prisoners home began. At that season of the year and with the scanty means-of convey-

---

[1] Mr. Dane and his colleague Mr. Barnard.

ance, even the journey to Salem and back to Andover was attended with no slight discomfort.

The following persons gave bonds for prisoners removed:

December 20, Dea. John Frye and Mr. John Osgood, for the appearance of Mary Osgood and Eunice Frye.

In October John Osgood and Nathaniel Dane had taken into custody the bodies of the children Dorothy and Abigail Faulkner, and January 13th, Francis Faulkner and John Marble gave bonds for their appearance. January 13th, John Osgood and John Barker gave bonds for William Barker and Mary Barker.

Francis Johnson and Walter Wright gave bonds for Stephen Johnson, about thirteen years old; Abigail Johnson about eleven years, Sarah Carrier about eight years. The same persons also gave bonds, five hundred pounds sterling, for John Sawdey, about thirteen years. This was a very large bond, two hundred pounds being the largest commonly paid. Hopestil Tyler and Jno. Bridges gave bonds for Martha Tyler and Joanna Tyler.

The efforts in behalf of those prisoners who were not allowed to be removed, had been so far successful that Governor Phipps ordered a session for the third of January of a "Court of Assizes and General Goal Delivery." The Court of Oyer and Terminer, before which the trials in the summer had been conducted, had then ceased to exist. The object of this court was to give verdict on the cases of those still in the jail and release the innocent from their confinement. Those in the foregoing list of names marked "not guilty" were the persons cleared at this court.

To attend this court as jurors four citizens of Andover were chosen.[1] The following is the warrant and return:

> These are in their Majestys names to Require you forthwith to assemble the free-holders and others the Inhabitants of your Towne who are hereby also required to choose foure good and Lawfull men of the

---

[1] *Mass. Archives vol. cxxxv., p. 92.*

same towne, each whereof to have a real estate of forty shillings per annum or a personal estate of fifty pounds, to serve as Jurors. Two upon the Grand Jury and two upon the Jury of Tryalls at a Court of Assizes and General Goal Delivery to be held at Salem for the County of Essex on Tuesday the third day of January next ensuing the days of the date hereof, which persons so chosen you are to summons to Attend the said Court by nine of the clock in the morning of ye said Day, and make returne hereof with the names of said p'sons the day before the said Court and hereof not to faile.

Dated in Boston the Twenty-third Day of December 1692.
To THE CONSTABLES OF ANDOVER OR EITHER OF THEM.

JONA. ELLARSON, CLERK.

In obedience unto this Above Riten Warant I have assembled the freeholders & others the Inhabitants of our Town Togither &; they have chosen Joseph Marble Snr &; Henry Holt snr, For the grand jury &; Left Christopher Osgood & Saml Osgood snr for the jury of Tryalls for sd above mentioned Cort & have sumoned them to Apeare according to Warents.

EPHRAIM FOSTER, CONSTABLE

The Rev. Mr. Dane addressed to this court a bold and firm but respectful letter, designed nominally to exculpate the town of Andover from blame, but really to condemn and discredit the "spectre-evidence" so largely relied on as ground of condemnation. It is a paper of special interest.[1]

Whereas there have been divers reports raysed, how and by what hands I know not, of the Towne of Andover and the Inhabitants, I thought it my bounden duty to give an account to others so farr as I had the understanding of anything amongst us. There-fore doe declare that I believe the reports have been scandalous and unjust, neither will bear ye light. As for that of the sieve and scissors, I never heard of it till this last summer, and the Sabbath after I spake publickly concerning it, since which I believe it hath not been tryed. As for such things of charms and wayes to find their cattle I never heard, nor doe I know any neighbors that ever did so, neither have I any grounds to believe it. I have lived above Fortie foure yeares in the Towne and have been frequent among ye Inhabitants and in my healthfull yeares oft at their habitations and should certainly heard if so it had been. That there was a suspicion of

---

[1] *Essex County Court Papers, "Witchcraft," vol. i, p. 142..*

Goodwife Carrier among some of us, before she was apprehended I know; as for any other persons I had no suspicion of them and had charity been put on, the Devil would not have had such advantage against us; and I believe many Innocent persons have been accused & Imprisoned; ye conceit of spectre evidence as an infallible mark did too far prevaill with us. Hence we so easily parted with our neighbors of an honest & good report & members in full communion; hence we so easily parted with our children when we knew nothing in their lives nor any of our neighbors to suspect them, and thus things were hurried on; hence such strange breaches in families; severall that came before me that spake with much sobrietie, professing their innocency, though through the devil's subtilty they were too much urged to confesse and we thought we did doe well in so doing; yet they stood their ground, professing their innocency; . . . . that they knew nothing; never saw ye devile, never made a covenant with him & ye like & some children that we have cause to feare that dread has overcome them to accuse themselves in that they knew not. Stephen Johnson, Mary Barker ye daughter of Leftenant Barker and some others by what we had from them with suitable assertions, we have come to believe they were in the truth and so held to it; if after many endeavors they had not been overcome to say what they never knew. This hath been a trouble to me, considering how oft it hath been sayd 'you are a witch,' 'you are guilty and who afflicts this maid,' or the like & more than this hath been said charging persons with witchcraft, and what flatteries have past from and threats and telling them they must goe to prison for it, &c., I feare have caused many to fall. Our sinne of Ignorance wherein we thought we did well will not excuse us, when we know we did amiss; but whatever might be a stumbling block to others must be removed, else we shall procure divine displeasure & evil will unavoidably brake in upon us.

> Your servant who am a friend though unworthie to them ye are friends to Sion.
>
> FRANCIS DANE, SNR

ANDOVER[1], Jan. 2, '92.

Concerning my daughter Elizabeth Johnson I never had ground to suspect her, neither have I heard any other accuse her, till by spectre evidence she was brought forth; but this I must say, she was weake and incapacious, fearfull, and in that respect I feare she hath falsely accused herself & others. Not long before she was sent for, she spake as to her owne particular that she was sure she was no witch, and for her Daughter Elizabeth she is but simplish at ye best, and I feare the common

---

[1] *This was 1693. The year did not begin till March, according to the old style of reckoning.*

speech that was frequently spread among us, of their liberty, if they would confesse and the like expression used by some have brought many into a snare. The Lord direct & guide those that are in place and give us all submissive wills & let the Lord doe with me and mine what seems good in his own eyes.

Mr. Dane also wrote to his brother ministers condemning in strong terms the belief in spectre-evidence, and all this combined with the influence of Mr. Simon Bradstreet, now one of the Assistants to Governor Phipps, helped to effect a change in the public sentiment and embolden to further effort. When the Court of Assize was held, a petition signed by fifty inhabitants of Andover was presented. It bore the names of thirty-eight men and twelve women:

> To THE HONOURED COURT OF ASSIZE HELD AT SALEM, the Humble Address of Several of the Inhabitants of Andover: May it please this Honored Court, we being sensible of the great sufferings our neighbors have been long under in prison and charitably judging that many of them are clear of that great transgression which hath been laid to their charge have thought it our duty to endeavor their vindication as far as our testimony for them will avail. The persons in whose behalf we are desired and concerned to speak something at present are Mrs. Mary Osgood, Eunice Frye, Deliverance Dane, Sarah Wilson, and Abigail Barker, who are women of whom we can truly give this character and commendation that they have not only lived among us so inoffensively as not to give the least occasion to any that know them to suspect them of witchcraft, but by their sober, godly and exemplary conversation have obtained a good report in the place where they have been well esteemed and approved in the church of which they are members.
>
> We were surprised to hear that persons of known integrity and piety were accused of so horrid a crime, not considering then that. the most innocent were liable to be so misrepresented and abused. When these women were accused by some afflicted, persons of the neighborhood their relations and others, though they had so good grounds of charity that they should not have thought any evil of them; yet, through a misrepresentation of the truth of that evidence that was so much credited and improved against people, took great pains to persuade them to own what they were by the afflicted charged with and indeed did unreasonably urge them to confess themselves guilty, as some of us who were then present can testify. But these good women did very much assert their innocency; yet some of them said they were not without fear lest Satan

had some way ensnared them because there was that evidence against them which then was by many thought to be a certain indication and discovery of witchcraft; yet they seriously professed they knew nothing by themselves of that nature. Nevertheless by the unwearied solicitations of those that privately discovered them both at home and at Salem they were at length persuaded publicly to own what they were charged with, and so submit to that guilt which we still hope and believe they are clear of. And it is probable that fear of what the event might be and the encouragement that it is said was suggested to them, that Confessing was the only way to obtain favor might be too powerful a temptation to timorous women to withstand in the hurry and distraction that we have heard they were then in. Had what they said against themselves pro ceeded from conviction of the fact we should have had nothing to have said for them; but we are induced to think that it did not, because they did soon privately retract what they had said, as we are informed, and while they were in prison they declared to such as they had confidence to speak freely and plainly to that they were not guilty of what they had owned and that what they had said against themselves was the greatest grief and burden they labored under.

Now though we cannot but judge it a thing very sinful for innocent persons to own a crime they are not guilty of, yet considering the well-ordered conversation of those women while they lived among us, and what they now seriously and constantly affirm in a more composed frame, we cannot but in charity judge them innocent of the great transgression that hath been imputed to them. As for the rest of our neighbors who are under the like circum- stances with these that have been named, we can truly say of them, that while they lived among us we have had no cause to judge them such persons as of late they have been represented to be, nor do we know that any of their neighbors had any just grounds to suspect them of that evil thing they are now charged with.

DUDLEY BRADSTREET.
FRANCIS DANE, SNR.
THOMAS BARNARD, AND OTHERS.

A carefully prepared petition signed by the accused women was also presented. This related the history of their arrest and trial; explained why they were ever led to confess, etc.:

.... Our nearest and dearest relations seeing us in that dreadful condition and knowing our great danger apprehended there was no other way to save our lives Indeed that confession that it is said we made was no other than what was suggested to us by some gentlemen, they telling us that we were witches and they knew it and we knew it, which made us think that it was so, and our understanding, our reason, our faculties almost gone, we were not capable of judging our condition. As also the hard measures they used with us rendered us incapable of making our defence, but said anything and everything which they desired, and with most of us what we said was but in effect a consenting to what they said.

The petition further says that, when the prisoners refused to confess, they were told to think of the fate of Wardwell who renounced his confession, and to remember that they would "goe after him."

The effect of these petitions on the court and the public, joined to the unwearied exertions of the Rev. Francis Dane, by private letters and solicitations to induce the clergy to discredit and condemn "spectre evidence," produced a strong reaction. Only a few persons were condemned in the trials of January, 1693, and these condemnations were, it is evident, simply for form's sake. The Andover prisoners released under bonds were not summoned to appear till May, just before the proclamation to open the prison doors and let the accused go free. Effectually to put an end to the delusion, and ensure the safety of the released, action for slander was brought against some of the accusers. These now doubly " afflicted " unfortunates, from having been objects of sensational curiosity and sympathy, became victims of public reproach and. odium. It was believed by many that they had been actuated by malicious motives, or instigated by the devil, to make the false charges.

One of these afflicted girls, Ann Putnam, of Salem (who had been at Andover, and had accused several citizens of the town of tormenting her, and Elizabeth Johnson of afflicting her with a spear), repented long and bitterly of her "sin." She was only twelve years of age at the time of the witch- craft, and when at twenty she sought refuge and peace of mind in the consolations and shelter of the church, her conscience (and probably the church officers) would not permit her to become a member until she had endured the humiliation of a public confession of her sin in the witchcraft accusations. Before the great congregation, which crowded to see and hear, she stood and gave her assent to the statement read by the minister:

"I desire to lie in the dust and to be humbled for it and earnestly beg forgiveness of God and from all those unto whom I have given just cause of offence whose relatives have been taken away or accused."

The indignation against the accusers, and the popular clamor for their punishment, seems in one of its aspects, almost as senseless as that had been against the accused; for it was really a renewal of the charge of witchcraft, now accusing the afflicted of having been influenced by the devil to make their first accusations. But the magistrates and ministers had no mind to reopen the question of Satanic agency, or possession of persons by evil spirits. Who was guilty and who was innocent, the wisest men in the colony thought best to leave to the judgments of Heaven and each man's own conscience.

How the good Judge Sewall viewed the part which he had taken in condemning the accused, and his yearly confession of the sin before the church, every reader of the colonial history knows. It is related by the poet who has immortalized so many New England names:

> Touching and sad a tale is told,
> Like a penitent hymn of the Psalmist old,
> Of the fast which the good man life long kept
> With a haunting sorrow that never slept,
> As the circling year brought round the time
> Of an error that left the sting of crime,
> When he sat on the bench of the witchcraft Courts
> With the laws of Moses and Hale's Reports,
> And spake, in the name of both, the word.
> That gave the witch's neck to the cord.
> And piled the oaken planks that pressed
> The feeble life from the warlock's breast.

One relic of the witchcraft delusion remains at North Andover, — the gravestone of a man who was said to have died by witchcraft:

TIMOTHY SWAN,[1]
DIED FEBRUARY YE 2 1692
AND IN YE 30 YEAR OF HIS AGE.

Some ten or more persons confessed to having " tortured, afflicted, consumed, wasted," this man. Three or four at a time, their spectres stood at his bedside and tortured him with iron spindles, pins, tobacco pipe, etc.

Andover as a community (both North and South Parishes), from that time to this, has been remarkably free from delusions and slow to be carried away by excitements, or frightened into panics.

As late as 1742 the church at Salem began to be again disturbed by such agitations, and at a church-meeting it was voted "that for Christians to seek to and consult reputed witches or fortune tellers is highly impious and scandalous."

But no such disposition appeared at Andover. Whether the experience of 1692 has served as a warning, or whether the fortresses of theology frowning down from the Hill have intimidated spiritual foes, or whether spectres yet appear on occasion to belated students and others, — Ichabod Cranes, along the lonely paths of Pomp's Pond, and the by-ways of Den Rock, and the roads by the Shawshin, or whether aerial broomsticks ever are visible to the young folks in their rides at eventide around Five-mile Pond, we leave to those who are versed in "witchcraft "to discover.

---

[1] *The Swan family were of Haverhill, but attended the North Church of Andover. Haverhill included a part of Methuen and a part of Lawrence.*

INDEX

A

Abbot, Benjamin 14, 15, 16
Abbot, John 33
Allen, Andrew 13, 26
Allen, John 13
Allen, Martha 13, 14
Aslebe, John 33

B

Ballard, John, the constable 9, 33
Ballard, Joseph 23
Ballard, wife of Joseph, of Andover 8
Barker, Abigail, wife of Ebenezer Barker 11, 46
Barker, Ebenezer 11, 34, 39
Barker, John 11, 43
Barker, Mary 43
Barker, Mary, single woman, daughter of John Barke 11
Barker, William 11, 22, 34, 43
Barnard, Thomas 9, 40, 47
Billerica, Mass. 13
Boston, Mass. 8
Boxford, Mass. 12, 22
Bradstreet, Dudley 10, 24, 37, 39, 47
Bradstreet, Mrs. Dudley 10
Bradstreet, Simon 42, 46
Brattle, Mr. of Boston 41
Bridges, John 39
Bridges, Jonathan 43
Bridges, Mary, Jr., daughter of 11
Bridges, Mary, wife of John Bridges 11
Bridges, Sarah, wife of Jo 11
Burroughs, Rev. George 18, 20, 26

C

Carrier, Andrew, son of Thomas Carrier 11
Carrier, Martha [Allen], wife of Thomas Carrier 11, 12, 13, 14, 16, 17, 18, 19, 20, 27, 31, 36, 45
Carrier, Richard, son of Thomas Carrier 11, 34
Carrier, Sarah, daughter of Thomas 11, 17
Carrier, Thomas 11
Carrier, Thomas, son of Thomas Carrier 11
Chandler, Phebe, daughter of William Chandler 16, 19
Chandler, Thomas 23
Chandler, William 16

D

Dane, Deliverance [Hazeltine], wife of Nathaniel 10, 11, 46
Dane, Elizabeth 33
Dane, Nathaniel 11, 39, 43
Dane, Rev. Francis 7, 9, 10, 18, 30, 35, 37, 40, 41, 44, 45, 46, 47, 48
Danvers, Mass. 7
Den Rock 50
Draper, John 11

E

Eames, Rebecca of Boxford 12
Ellarson, Jonathan, Clerk 44
Emerson, John 35

F

Farnum, John, son of Ralph Farnum Snr 16

Farnum, Ralph Jnr. 16
Farnum, Ralph, Snr. 16
Farrington, Edward 11
Faulkner, Abigail
   10, 11, 28, 29, 30, 37, 43
Faulkner, Dorothy 10, 11, 43
Faulkner, Francis 11, 30, 43
Fawkes, Sarah, single woman, wife of
   Francis Johns 11
Five-mile Pond 9, 34, 50
fortune-telling 7, 24
Foster, Abraham 11
Foster, Andrew 16
Foster, Ann 11, 18, 25, 26, 27, 31
Foster, Ephraim 23
Frye, Deacon John
   11, 34, 39, 41, 43
Frye, Eunice 10, 11, 43, 46
Frye, Samuel 33

G

Gedney, Bartholomew 37
ghost story-telling 7
Godfrey, John 6, 7

H

Hathorne, John 37
Haverhill 7
Holt, Henry, Snr. 44
Holt, Samuel 13
Holt, Samuel Snr. 16
Houlton, Joseph 14
Howard, Nathan 32
Hubbard, Elizabeth 15

J

Johnson, Abigail 12, 33
Johnson, Elizabeth
   10, 11, 30, 31, 45
Johnson, Elizabeth, Jnr. 10, 30, 31

Johnson, Francis 11, 12, 30, 33, 43
Johnson, John 12
Johnson, Rebecca 12
Johnson, Stephen 11, 12, 30, 33, 43
Johnson, Stephen, Jr. 33
Johnson, Thomas 40

L

Lacey, Lawrence 12
Lacey, Mary [Foster]
   11, 12, 18, 28, 31
Lacey, Mary, Jnr. 12, 18
Lovejoy, John 26

M

Marble, John 43
Marble, Joseph Snr. 44
Marston, John 34, 39
Marston, Mary 34, 39
Mather, Rev. Cotton 8, 17, 20
Mather, Rev. Increase 35, 36

N

Newbury falls 31
Noyes, Rev. Mr. 25

O

Osgood, Christopher 39, 44
Osgood, John 12, 34, 39, 40, 41, 43
Osgood, Mary 10, 12, 34, 36, 43, 46
Osgood, Samuel 44

P

palmistry 7
Parker, Joseph 12
Parker, Mary 11, 12, 21, 22
Parker, Sarah 12
Parker, sons of Mary 21
Phelps, Sarah 30

Phipps, Gov. Wm. 43, 46
Pomp's Pond 50
Poor, Daniel 33
Post, Mary, of Boxford, daughter of Rebecca Johns 12
Preston, John 11
Preston, Samuel 19
Preston, Samuel Jnr. 16
Putnam, Ann 8, 31, 48

R

Roger, John 19

S

Salem village 7, 9, 14, 18, 35, 37, 46
Sawdey, John 12
Sewall, Samuel 49
Sewall, Stephen, Clerk 16
Shawshin River 9, 24, 50
Sheldon, Susan 15
sleight-of-hand tricks 7
Sprague, Martha of Boxford 22, 23, 30
Stevens, John 33
Swan, Timothy 22, 26, 50

T

Toothaker, Allen 13, 16, 19
Toothaker, Mary 13
Toothaker, Roger of Ipswich and Billerica 13
Tyler, Goody 12, 34, 35
Tyler, Hannah 34
Tyler, Hopestil 12, 39, 43
Tyler, Job of Boxford 7
Tyler, Johanna 29
Tyler, Johanna, daughter of Hopestil Tyler 12, 43
Tyler, Joseph 29
Tyler, Martha 29, 43

Tyler, Mary, wife of Hopestil Tyler 12

W

Walcott, John of Salem 14
Wardwell, Mercy, daughter of Samuel Wardwell 12, 22, 34
Wardwell, Samuel 11, 12, 22, 23, 25, 32, 33
Wardwell, Sarah 11, 12, 32, 33
Willard, John 20
Williams, Abigail 15
Williard, John 20
Wilson, Joseph 12, 39
Wilson, Sarah 12, 29, 46
Wright, Walter, Constable 14, 43

www.ingramcontent.com/pod-product-compliance
Lightning Source LLC
Chambersburg PA
CBHW031434040426
42444CB00006B/804